MAN'S GREAT AWAKENING

MAN'S
GREAT
AWAKENING

(Beautiful Mud)

W. BALLENTINE HENLEY

Science of Mind Publications
Los Angeles, California

First Printing — January 1974

Second Printing — May 1974

Published by SCIENCE OF MIND PUBLICATIONS
3251 West Sixth Street P.O. Box 75127
Los Angeles, California 90075

DEDICATED

To Ernest Holmes,
who inspired the original concept in 1932
and
To my wife, Helen,
who gently insisted that
the manuscript be completed

CONTENTS

Foreword 9

Preface 11

I   Beautiful Mud 13

II   Beginnings..15

III   The Origins of Social Law 25

IV   Law, the Balance 37

V   Science, the Seeker...................................45

VI   Spirit and Essence 61

VII   Religion, the Flower.................................65

VIII   The Endless Journey 85

FOREWORD

Here is the story of where man has been, where
he is today, and a glimpse of his possible future.
The story is every man's story, for he is born of the
past, and is parent to the future.

Dr. W. Ballentine Henley is known to countless
thousands across the country and around the
world, and his talk, "Beautiful Mud," has fasci-
nated all. This book is an extension of the ideas in
that talk. The holder of many degrees, he is an
eminent educator.

After an outstanding career as Provost of the
College of Medicine, University of California,
Irvine, he retired and then became President of the
United Church of Religious Science, which was
founded by the late Dr. Ernest Holmes. Since his
early teens he knew and was associated with Dr.
Holmes.

Contained in this volume are ideas that have

grown and developed through the years concerning the nature and destiny of man. In spite of some appearances to the contrary the author has implicit faith in the inner nature of man, the spiritual essence of man, to carry him on to greater and greater stages of development.

Even though we seem to know considerable about man's past, and the direction of his growth in the future, it seems impossible to forecast what man may yet be. But there is an infinite potential within him that can lead him to a future un-dreamed of today.

Willis Kinnear
Director
Science of Mind Publications

PREFACE

This is a brief survey of the nature of man and a glimpse of some of the forces which have molded him into his present expression of life. Through a few bright examples of history's immortal men, it weaves the living threads of law, science, and religion into the cable which has lifted man out of the past to a place from which he can aspire to mingle with the stars.

Man's conscious creative powers are the fluorescence of millions and billions of years of matter and life evolving into finer structures and states of being. The qualities which make man human—different from all other animals—are the spiritual, intellectual, and cultural qualities which have at their pinnacle the ability to love and be loved.

The radiance of men of the past, and those who live today, is but the finite manifestation of the

Infinite. Science now, as never before in history, is giving us the evidence to believe this.

W.B.H.

I

BEAUTIFUL MUD

A story about Bishop Quale, "The Skylark of Methodism," was a favorite of Dr. M. S. Rice. Bishop Quale loved nature in all her moods, and one rainy day Dr. Rice accompanied him on a walk. They came to a small stream and paused on its bank.

"Isn't it beautiful!" the bishop exclaimed, as he took off his shoes and socks to wade about in it. He scooped up a clot of mud and holding it in the air he said, "Look at it. Isn't it wonderful? It is the symbol of utmost sacrifice. It is the attrition of the rocks over thousands of ages; the dead and decaying forms of millions of plants that have died to give new fresh life to the world." Then he picked a white flower from the stream bank and holding both the flower and the mud in the air he said, "Truly, beautiful mud!"

A tourist whose car is mired to its hubcaps

beside a muddy Kansas roadside would not see beauty in the gooey mass which works its way between tire and fender as a man with a tractor or a team of horses pulls him to drier ground. It is a question of appreciation, and of attitude.

One day at a London gallery where the works of William Turner were on exhibit a little cluster of critics stood before a painting of a basket of fruit with a dragonfly poised on the handle. "I'm sure I've never seen a dragonfly in such outlandish colors," sniffed one. Another said that its head was not well-done, and they all agreed that the wings were too long. In the midst of the discussion the dragonfly lifted its wings and sped out the window. The critics had been finding fault with the only real thing in the picture.

When we read the New Testament passage in which Herod sets Jesus at naught, it becomes plain that on that day Herod placed judgment not upon Jesus, but upon Herod. His bid for immortality was the great blunder that he made. Our censures and judgments of the world are not so much a depreciation of the world as a confession of our own standards of appreciation. The challenges and crises of today make it important to occasionally seek a new perspective. There are signs of regeneration in the air for those who wish to see them.

II

BEGINNINGS

A fascinating hypothesis has been advanced in the realm of speculative science. Sight is the eye's perception of light rays reflected by objects. It has been proposed that once the light rays are set in motion through infinite space they are, perhaps, caused to curve back toward the Earth. The suggestion is that man may someday invent a device which will collect those rays. Just as we now use radio and television, so in time we may be able to tune in on past centuries. If we could buy or borrow such an instrument we could observe some wonderful and terrible things.

When we talk of the age of the Earth as being from four to five billion years, we may recall an old controversy. The age of the Earth, before the development of the carbon 14 dating process, had been estimated at anywhere from 10 million to 100 billion years. The age of a rock—perhaps a sedimentary rock containing fossils—is measured by the proportion of lead isotopes into which its radioactive elements have decayed. Samples have been found indicating an age of 4.5 billion years for our planet, but this does not account for the elements of which the planet was constructed. It is supposed that the basic elements are from one to 1.5 billion years older than the planet itself.

Suppose that we could tune a light-ray machine to a channel five billion years old. The machine would show us a mass of gaseous substance expanding and contracting. The centuries, passing swiftly, present a panorama of geological changes preparing the Earth for life.

The first picture is of roiling flame and exploding gases, and then the machine lets us see a layer of sediment forming on the surface of the small, tight cloud of matter. The lifeless Archeozoic Era has begun. The scene changes continuously, slowly, to the Proterozoic Era. Here the earliest traces of life emerge, under an atmosphere denser than ours today. Massive clouds obscure the sun. Volcanoes spit fire and liquid rock into the air, breaking the skyline in places, interrupting the monotony of the barren soilless landscape.

Then the rainstorms begin. The rain sweeps sediment into the sea where it forms marine ledges and flats, which will harden into slate, sandstone, and limestone and preserve the story of emerging life in solid rock. Soft, infinitesimal, jellylike masses reproduce and display the mysterious quality called life. It is during these long days that life begins to wiggle in the mud.

The first amphibious creatures became stranded in the pools formed at the edge of the sea in the Proterozoic Era and left their prints in the young rocks of the Paleozoic Era while they developed the ability to breathe air. The Paleozoic was a period of life's adaptation to the different parts of the total environment. It was followed by the Mesozoic Era in which the great reptiles flourished but failed to make adjustments to their world which would have enabled them to survive.

By the next age, the Cenozoic, the Earth was conditioned for a new type of living matter, and at this juncture the ancestor of man and of mammals made its appearance.

"And from the remote mists of Time there emerged some solitary humanoid creatures who started a hard, wandering life over the face of the earth. Between these the first prehistoric men—polished links in a long biological chain—and the original amorphous amoeba there already existed a distance of millions of years." Thus Dr. Felix Martí-Ibañez begins *The Epic of Medicine*.

The most distant ancestors of man and the apes

lived in North Africa about 23 million years ago. These creatures, called hominoids, formed the main line that branched into hominids, man's direct ancestors, and pongids, the ape's precursors. The hominid branch probably occurred in the late Miocene period, which lasted between 25 and 10 million years ago, developed into the australopithecine stage and finally the hominine state in man's development.

Like a surviving patriarch, 14-million-year-old Ramapithecus appeared to be the oldest human ancestor until a specimen thought to be six million years his senior was found on Victoria Island in Kenya by the venerable Dr. L.S.B. Leakey, Kenyan anthropologist and archeologist. Almost simultaneously the evolutionary chain was strengthened by the discovery in Kenya of an arm bone fragment belonging to Ramapithecus' only known descendant, 2.5-million-year-old Australopithecus. The gap of millions of years in man's genus branch from Ramapithecus to Advanced Australopithecus was slightly narrowed by the find of the arm bone fragment whose onetime possessor, by virtue of his extraordinary age, became the oldest of his group of known descendants.

Our light-ray machine gives us a picture of the early Australopithecus, and we can see that youth endowed him with scant charm. He appears to be about four feet tall, with human-like teeth and upright stance. His jawbone is thick and heavy, and we know that he had a small, apelike brain. His predecessors, after all, included Ramapithecus and Kenyapithecus, who, though hominidae—members of the family of man—were too much the ape to be called "men." Small comfort to them that the family of man did not include any genuine apes, but only a common ancestor! We would not have known from seeing him on our screen that Homo habilis, at 1,750,000 years the oldest member of the human genus, was not an ape, had not the tireless Dr. and Mrs. Leakey found his remains in the Olduvai Gorge of Tanzania.

Seitz writes in *American Science* that the most critical part of man's evolution from earlier forms occurred in the last two to three million years, during which man developed four important characteristics: toolmaking, speech, group cooperation, and the ability to reason logically. Toolmaking implies the intelligent use of objects, and vocabulary is a part of speech development. Group cooperation stemmed from social maturation. The ability to reason logically is the most vital factor setting man apart from other forms of life.

For centuries early man struggled in the life-giving mud, unconsciously striving to sculpt it into the image of his dreams. It is one of the mistaken concepts of dawn man that he had much of the spiritual equipment of modern man. Tennyson wrote, "The Lord let the house of a brute to the soul of man." In Genesis we are told that Adam, a brute, did not know good from evil. It is submitted that he was thus a perfect brute. Evolution has caused some little change in the housing, but the mentality that animates it has changed from the instincts of a brute to the reasoning mind of man.

We find traits of animal, child, savage, and modern adult comprising the civilized man, and an entire science has been evolved around each. Human learning develops due to man's ability to notice distinctions and analyze situations, and his methods of transmitting the information to others. Learning in life's lower ranks is individual and not cooperative; a monkey learns by monkeying and seldom, if ever, apes. History and change have been made possible by a small number of prophets, who were really gropers and monkeyers, whose curiosity outran that of their fellows and allowed them to escape from the errors of those around them. It is said that if the lives of 300 men were deleted from their particular places in history man would be back in the predawn ages.

In *The Mind in the Making* James Harvey Robinson has reduced the entire history of man into a time span that is easier to grasp, by pretending that in 50 years a single generation of men has accomplished all that which now passes for civilization. On a 50-year scale they would have taken the first 49 years to acquire the intelligence to forego their nomadic habits and settle down to plant crops, domesticate animals, and create clothing and tools for themselves. The first six months of the 50th year would have been marked by the invention of writing, which enabled men to establish a means of spreading and perpetuating civilization. By the ninth month literature, art, and philosophy have reached a high degree of refinement. For the last two months men have been living under the benevolence of Christianity. The printing press is two weeks old and the steam engine but seven days. For two or three days people have been traveling the Earth in steamships and railway cars, and only yesterday they discovered electricity. Within the last few hours they learned to fly through the air, even to the moon, and to navigate under the sea. They turned their arts and sciences to prosecuting several magnificent wars befitting certain of their ideas and consuming quantities of their resources. Robinson asks us not to be disappointed at this last tendency, because only a week ago men were boiling their political opponents in oil and burning old women as witches for trafficking with the devil.

If all the bits of history could be gathered together, the trails would lead back to a group of half-human creatures seeking, in fear, ignorance, and confusion, to become men. Their progress has been highlighted as well as made possible by the fearless, free-flying minds of courageous individuals. The man who felled a tree and rolled it to the water's edge, then hollowed it out and laboriously launched it, fathered every proud vessel now on the sea. Thousands of years ago an inspired genius fashioned a wheel from the stump of a tree, and man has been rolling along ever since.

The old man of the tribe who held up ten fingers to indicate the number of enemies he killed that day started a system that made possible the measurement of the distances between stars. Lynn Harold Hough emphasizes the importance of this discovery. The first shepherd who realized that he had as many sheep as he had fingers was on the way to abstract thinking. Even today we are told that a genius is one who can count to 20 without using his toes. When the idea of ten became separate from the fingers, man found himself possessed of the power of abstract reasoning.

Pierre Teilhard de Chardin, the Jesuit priest, who, as a paleontologist and biologist, was the predominant figure in the discovery of Peking man, has written that we have reached a point in our human evolution at which we must cease to resort to violent means for achieving social order. We must be prepared, he writes, to accept and embrace as necessary and inevitable the power and the effects of Love, universal.

III

THE ORIGINS
OF SOCIAL LAW

Three intellectual processes have had a compelling influence on civilization. They are law, science, and religion.

The first continuous legal system, established in 2510 B.C., was Chinese, and the second was the Code of Hammurabi, inscribed in stone about 2100 B.C. 1200 B.C. is usually accepted as the date of the Mosaic Code. In 600 B.C. the Greeks developed the first secular code, called the Laws of Solon, and Confucius was chief justice in China 100 years later. The next milestone was reached 550 years after the birth of Jesus when Emperor Justinian ordered all the laws of the Roman Empire to be codified.

When moral law set itself firmly behind any legal system it gave that system more strength and stability than statutes alone could have given. Man tends to act from his inherited training, and his earliest society was the family. When families banded together into tribes, tribal property and family property became institutions. With each step into a larger community, the idea that one had rights to his own personal belongings became stronger.

Law is the outgrowth of social interaction, of man's association with others. First, man developed a language, then he learned to reason, and then he began to reflect. Soil cultivation and animal husbandry created the concept of property and property rights, and increased the food supply so that man could live in communities. As populations in the primary areas of settlement became denser, men began to need definitions of individual and collective rights and regulation of conduct.

In his *The Story of Law* John M. Zane reconstructs the origins of social law. Because man was moved by a basic gregariousness, or herd instinct, the survival of all depended upon uniformity of action. Kant mistakenly thought himself the discoverer of the precept that one should so act that the rule of his action could become the general law. When a judge enjoins a jury to consider whether or not the defendant exercised that degree of care which the average prudent man would use under the circumstances, the judge is echoing the rule established by his ancestors. Early law was merely the formal delineation, often in writing, of matters that were already custom and usage.

The written law was venerated as unchangeable divine law delivered from a god to the king of the city, as among the Babylonians, whose written language led to the use of documents in the form of inscribed clay tablets or stone which became the means of defining the application of the law. Courts were instituted by many early cultures for the decision of controversies, and citizens had the choice to use or not use them. Formal division of powers as we know it today had not come into being. The king, who usually was either the representative, the incarnation, or the mouthpiece of the god, still had all powers if he cared to exercise them.

The Jews and the tribes of Israel typify the development of law. Moses presented the Ten Commandments as the laws of God dictated by God, and they were accepted as guides of conduct, but they were evolved by the prophets as reflections of moral principles in which individual responsibility received increasing emphasis.

Like most early systems of law, the Ta Tsing Leu Lee was integrated with the religious customs and procedures of the strict family structure of

China. It was the code of fundamental Chinese law. First framed in rather primitive form around 2150 B.C., it matured during the Tsing Dynasty in the mid-17th Century B.C., and has lasted until recently.

The administrative, criminal, and civil sections of the Ta Tsing Leu Lee were repealed upon the formation of the republic. The temporary criminal code was adopted in 1912, but the civil section of the old system was not replaced until 1929 or 1930. The new civil code skirted the principles of religion when it prescribed the honor and commemoration citizens must pay genii of nature, the enlightened emperor, his venerable ancestors, ministers and sages. One hundred blows were ordered as punishment for failure to perform the rites and procedures properly.

China's culture flourished in such isolation, and the Chinese language has such unique qualities, that it is fair to say that the Ta Tsing Leu Lee was not a great influence upon the refinement of the Western system of law.

It was the mud, teeming with life, out of which Western civilization and law were born. The Nile spawned a sophisticated civilization in Egypt, and the "fertile crescent" of the Tigris and Euphrates Rivers produced the remarkable Sumerians and Chaldeans, and the Babylonians whose king,

Hammurabi, gave the most to legal history.

In some libraries the attention of visitors is often drawn to an appropriate corner in which stands a black stone, a replica of the eight-foot stele on which the Code of Hammurabi was inscribed in about the year 2100 B.C. When the stone was found at Susa in 1902 it was described as a complete and perfect monument to the laws of ancient Babylonia, and an influence on the laws of Israel. It had been used and studied for more than 1500 years.

Whether it was original or a compilation of contemporary usage, the Code of Hammurabi transcended mere tribal custom, recognizing neither blood feud, private retribution, nor marriage by capture. It reidentified the king as the source of justice. Judges were strictly supervised and the king held the prerogative of appeal. Babylonians enjoyed the services of a postal system, police, and masters of the levees, and there was a feudal landing system.

The Code of Hammurabi divided the population into three groups. The Awelu, the upper class, compensated for its aristocratic privileges with the highest monetary and religious responsibilities. The Muskinu group appears to have encompassed the bulk of the population. The Muskinu were free, and their fees, fines, and religious duties were smaller than those of the Awelu. The Ardu caste was chattel. Oddly enough, an Ardu could acquire property and hold other slaves, but his social obligations rested upon his master.

The earliest inhabitants of the Tigris-Euphrates valley, the Sumerians, built great cities and maintained their records with care. Their transactions in land, property, and slaves were inscribed on clay tablets which have been preserved. Some of their laws represent attempts to impose respect for older customs and to curb the rapacity of priests and officials guilty of extortion from the poor.

The Euphrates River changed course in about 3300 B.C., leaving the Sumerian capital of Kish, to flow beside the city of Babylon. Babylon was famed for its astrologers and astronomers, especially in the reign of Nebuchadnezzar. They recorded the rising and setting of Venus, the orbits and eclipses of the Sun and Moon, the planets' courses, the difference between planets and stars, and they determined the solstices and equinoxes. The 60-second minute and the 60-minute degree, the waterclock, the sundial, and the perfection of metallurgy are to their credit.

The first actual records of court proceedings are from the Chaldean capital of Ur. These documents, all from about 2100 B.C., begin with the phrase "Judgment rendered." They describe disputes arising from sales and inheritances, divorces and gifts. The courts were presided over by two watchers, one of whom might be a city governor or a royal delegate. Claims were sometimes made in the name of the king. In approximately 2000 B.C. Sumerian family law came into being, regulating adoption, relationship of parent to child, divorce, hiring of slaves, and services.

In ancient Egypt which, like Babylon, was dependent on the rich river mud, the pharaoh was the fountainhead of law and justice. Deified by birth and by his royal office, he was not worshipped in the temple only, but in the courts and lodgings of his kingdom. Egypt under the pharaohs progressed from a neolithic culture to a nation familiar with hieroglyphic writing on papyrus, metals, and colored glass. A caste of scribes became the first physicians and the death-obsessed Egyptians chronicled diseases and therapies in medical papyri antedating the *Corpus Hippocraticum* by 1200 years.

Egyptian governmental structure in the Old Kingdom achieved an elaborate condition of state functioning under local officials, a condition unparalleled in Europe until the latter years of the Roman Empire. James Henry Breasted, the Egyptologist, says that the actual laws of ancient Egypt have never been discovered, though some facts about them are known. Judging, it is believed, was a part of the administrative duties of governors and officials supposedly learned in the law, rather than a separate profession. The pharaoh's vizier, who often served as chief justice, was the immediate head of the organization of government, and the most powerful official next to the pharaoh himself. The laws, attributed to the gods, were contained in forty scrolls which were placed by requirement on the dais at the vizier's public sessions, that the law might be accessible to any who wished to consult it.

The scrolls have vanished, but the law contained within them is reputed to have been just and impartial. It is interesting to note that even conspirators against the pharaoh's life were not summarily put to death. Legally constituted court proceedings were provided where a proper trial could be obtained, and the accused was condemned only if found guilty.

Egyptian and Babylonian law contributed significantly to the flowering of Mosaic law in which law and religion were again closely intertwined. The blossoms of Israel's legal system were the Ten Commandments.

Each commandment was a bright center petaled by similar regulations. The commandments served as a basis for both religious and civil conduct.

They carried no sanctions within themselves, because the people were told by their leaders what the punishments would be. The old ideas of general liability rather than individual responsibility were an intrinsic part of Israelite law.

The Greek system of jurisprudence was simple and drastically democratic. A panel of freemen heard individuals plead their cases, and then they voted. Aryan customs of tribal or public assembly were maintained. Legislative, judicial, and administrative matters were decided in this assembly, which was rather like a large oligarchy, excluding the many slaves and resident aliens from participation. Because the assembly represented the democratic ideal that any citizen was capable of governing, it selected public officers by lot. Even Solon, the great lawgiver, was chosen in this manner.

The Greek legal system was most unique in its practice of determining a law in consequence, rather than in anticipation, of actions. Its greatest failure was the lack of either a competent judicial tribunal or legislative power, or a legal system made up of a quorum of men devoted to the science, study, and application of the rules of law. The Hellenic system was later used by the Romans.

The experiences of Babylonia, Israel, and Greece contributed to Roman law. Rome gave the civilized world principles of law and order and was made the center of the world's affairs. It was in Rome that a clearly defined legal profession, equipped with competent tribunals, introduced juristic methods in upholding law. Roman law was created by Roman courts and professional jurists and advocates. Greek citizens below the rank of noble had once demanded a written body of law that all could read and learn, and later in Rome a committee of ten men engraved the laws on brass and called it the Twelve Tables.

In the 6th Century A.D. the Emperor Justinian gathered all the legal accumulations of the past into the code which is known by his name. It was assembled just in time; the barbarian hordes were ramming the walls of Rome. There were those who believed that Roman civlization would first crumble within, but the barbarian sacking of Rome brought the descent of the dark. Civilization moved into the period called, in some cases erroneously, the Dark Ages. The culture and the stable institutions of the past retreated to monastic sanctury. Some of the monasteries on the distant island of Britain, where some semblance of order was maintained, preserved the light of learning in monastery windows.

When William the Conqueror crossed the English Channel in 1066 he found in the land the laws of

Angles, Saxons, Danes, and Jutes. In the monasteries he found the remnants of ecclesiastical law, containing the laws of ancient Rome as found in the Justinian code.

Wisely, the Norman conquerors did not disrupt the local courts. Instead, they instituted an elaborate system of king's justice. This design was not without fault. In order to gain access to the superior brand of justice dispensed by the king's courts, one had to obtain the proper writ, which could be had for a fee. The law's complexity or the incompetence of the lawyer made pleading such a technical maze that justice often went begging.

To remedy these shortcomings, the king selected the most prominent lawyer from the ecclesiastical courts and made him chancellor. The office of chancellor involved, in effect, being custodian of the king's conscience, and its title was derived from the name of the screen behind which the officer sat when he heard cases. Out of these chancellery hearings the principles of equity were evolved.

When the colonists emigrated to America they brought the written and unwritten laws of England and the principles of equity. In their own time and from their own experience they compiled the Constitution of the United States. After it came tribunals and codes and systems of administrative laws.

IV

LAW, THE BALANCE

Animal life on earth before the coming of man had a social organization superior in its continuity to that which man has developed. The Proverbs say, "Go to the ant, thou sluggard; consider her ways and be wise." It might have said the same of the bee. And yet, there is no place for change in either social group. Caring for the young and gathering food for the community are the primary concerns. Each ant or bee acts as if its action could become a general rule of conduct, a guiding principle which appears in the early development of human law.

These creatures were living on the earth long before man, and perhaps they will be here when man is gone. Many theorists, including communists, have used these communal dwellings as a model of an ideal society. In the anthill and beehive cleanliness of the person and of the living area is so important that refuse is constantly being removed. Every individual has access to the community property. There is no private ownership, even of young.

These qualities have made survival possible for millions of years. They have also made it impossible for ants and bees to evolve into anything else. With innovation and change nonexistent, the fundamental nature of the human mind as evolved through centuries has no place in the anthill or beehive.

Animalistic learning still exists among men. The security of having survived yesterday encourages a tendency to do today as one did before; there could be no better guarantee that one will survive today than if he follows the procedure which meant survival in the past.

Man began as an animal, responding primarily to his environment. Soon he became differentiated from the animal in his ability to change. He can think about what he is doing; he can invent new techniques. He can change his own personality, character, and behavior. In the animal world the social structure creates the individual, while the individual in the human world can shape the social structure and mold the law. Man is an animal passing slowly from the brutal, instinctive stage to the rational, conceptual, thoughtful stage. He has been able to rise above the sensual world and perceive a spiritual power that seemed to make him kin to something beyond himself.

Law is the social balance. The important part of a watch is not the mainspring but the balance wheel. Law performs as a stabilizing force upon the ways of men by attempting to put "the rule of law, and not of men" upon their actions. Without the rule of law, anarchy befouls society with retrogression, decay, and disintegration. The story of the rise and fall of civilizations is also the story of the adherence to or departure from the great principles. Law is the regulatory power which prevents the pendulum of time and change from swinging to an extreme in either direction.

Law is sometimes defined as an established rule. The laws of physical science and the laws of human action are the two divisions of established rule.

The term "laws" as used in physical science is probably a misnomer from the standpoint of jurisprudence. Physical laws are merely the observed uniformities. For instance, whenever an apple becomes detached from a tree it falls to the ground, thus proving the law of gravitation. The law of jurisprudence considers that the individual has the power of discretion to obey or disobey, while the laws or principles governing physical nature have to do with objects which are powerless to shape their own courses of action or intelligently direct their destinies. What we observe as law in physical science is really order within nature. Certain results always follow certain causes in nature, a property which seems to be the essential quality of matter. The detached apple has no power to choose whether or not it shall fall, but must comply with the principles which govern the universe.

Human law is sometimes defined as a rule of *Human Conduct* proscribed by the supreme power of a state, commanding what is right and prohibiting what is wrong, and enforced by the sanctioning powers of the sovereign state. A sanction is sometimes regarded as that power which compels obedience, when obedience is not the unavoidable consequence. In this, the distinction between natural and human law is made a little plainer.

There are other confusions and misapplications of the term "law" beyond such stretched analogies as "obeying the laws of nature." When the "laws" of economics or of sociology are cited, the term means the formulation of certain tendencies, rather than rigid ordinances. It does not imply an imperative, because there has not been enough experimentation in the social sciences to permit appropriate controls to be set up for accurate observation of the uniformities of compliance. Furthermore, once social tendencies are manifested they are subject to modification under changing conditions. For this reason, the laws of mechanics and economics and the laws of morality are frequently confused. In the normative sciences such as ethics, logic, and aesthetics, the term "law" is used in the sense of a regulative ideal. In ethics, for example, law is concerned with what ought to be done and not with the facts of the action itself.

I used to ask my students of jurisprudence to fold their hands together and note which thumb is on top, and then unclasp their hands, repeat the action and place the other thumb on top. This caused them a strange sensation. Once in babyhood they folded their hands and made the great decision of which thumb should go on top, and the one chosen had been there ever since. The rule of habit determines whether we put on the right or left shoe first every morning, and which way to drive to the office, campus, or market, though it was not an easy task to decide the first time on the best places to turn. This is a commonplace demonstration of *stare decisis*—the rule of the decision— which means that it is inevitable that one decision becomes a precedent to be upheld in human conduct, and in law.

Formulae and written laws were preceded by

custom and usage, which had the same compelling power. The constraining force in ancient custom was ostracism from the group. Man is a social animal, as Aristotle said, and so this coercion has been influential from the beginning of time. Morals, customs, and usage crystallize into written laws and ordinances when society becomes more formalized.

Law is not static. It moves surely, though slowly. As men by strange instinct fix upon higher values and worthier goals, they will change the social structure and improve the environment. Change in the law is not effected by violent destruction of the law, but by orderly processes established by the community to facilitate progress. Progress is not based on the assumption that to improve one must first destroy and then build on the ashes. This wasteful philosophy risks destruction so great that society may suffer loss before the rebuilding takes place. A type of intelligence has evolved in man which is capable of infinite expansion and of overcoming natural barriers and surroundings, a process which makes it possible for man and his social structures to be constantly perfecting themselves and establishing fresh goals.

In the comprehensive view of the development of law one can see an unceasing elaboration which is sometimes by the creative thought of one individual, but rather often by those inarticulate millions of human beings who, though they remain unrecognized by history, help construct civilization and are essential to the progress of man. John M. Zane states it this way in his *The Story of Law:*

"It is a sound corrective to our thinking to remember, in the words of a great scientist, that 'what we are is in part only of our own making; the greater part of ourselves has come down to us from the past.' What we know and what we think is not a new fountain gushing fresh from the barren rock of the unknown at the stroke of the rod of our own intellect; it is a stream which flows by us and through us, fed by the far-off rivulets of long ago. As what we think and say to-day will mingle with and shape the thoughts of men in the years to come, so in the opinions and views which we are proud to hold to-day we may, by looking back, trace the influence of the thoughts of those who have gone before. It is in the history of law, far more than in any other social science, that we catch from its very beginning the great corporate life of humanity which has made us what we are."

V

SCIENCE, THE SEEKER

Science is the second strand in the cable woven by man as he struggled to lift himself out of the mud. Man first surveyed his universe with wonder and then he began to ask questions which he sought to answer by assembling facts and attempting to generalize upon them. For centuries his generalizations involved imagination and superstition, but from the very beginning he displayed the capacities to reason, to question, and to analyze. Only recently has man discovered his natural gift for thinking in abstractions.

If you and I had visited Egypt after one of the Nile floods some 2500 years ago we might have seen this talent for abstraction at its best in a visitor from Greece. He stood on the bank of the Nile watching Egyptians relocating boundaries by lining up points on one side of the river with points on the other side. To the observant Greek their

work represented something vastly more important. He described it in such sentences as "A
straight line is the shortest distance between two
points," and a host of other challenging propo-
sitions which have given students headaches ever
since. The visitor was Thales, the father of modern
geometry. He not only measured the diameter of
the Sun but predicted its eclipse, and he suggested
the constellation of Ursa Minor, the "Little Bear,"
as a guide for nautical navigation.

Across the Mediterranean, Greek philosophy and
science reached their apex during the Hippocratic
Revolution. In this, a time named for a man born
into a family of physician-priests in 460 B.C.,
medicine took great steps toward becoming a
science.

Hippocrates' concept of medical ethics enhanced
the stature of the profession. His clarification of
various attitudes toward the "ideal" physician and
the physician's approach to medicine resulted in a
code of ethics which reprehends advertising, ex-
ploitation of patients, violation of the patient-
doctor relationship, and the confidential nature of
the physician. He was not only the first in Greek
history to regulate the quality and standards of
physicians, but his action was the first self-
regulatory attempt by physicians which was not
compelled by the state. One of Hippocrates' final

legacies was his practice of keeping case histories.

To the extent that Hippocrates was able to exclude both religion and philosophy from his medical observations, he may be said to have staged a revolution. He taught that diseases have natural courses which the physician must know thoroughly in order to be able to decide whether the outcome would be favorable or fatal. The basic concept of his teachings was that the physician does not fight nature but tries to aid her in effecting a natural cure by removing the regimen which might hinder normal recovery. This, of course, is one of the motivating factors in modern medicine. He applied his concepts through the use of the inductive scientific method, which was also quite out of keeping with the medical practice of his time.

Hippocrates was born into a world in which Aesculapius was the god of medicine. Hippocrates never believed that the gods sent or removed illnesses, and so he was in opposition to a powerful cult. At one time in Greece and Rome there were over 200 temples of Aesculapius. Patients went to centers to spend the night and the priests walked among them, appearing to the sick as reincarnations of the god. They prescribed medications and treatments, and certainly they practiced psychotherapy and an amount of religious persuasion. Through their accumulated experiences in watching the sick for a night or more prior to treatment the priests became fairly expert at diagnosis. Hippocrates, who lived and taught near the center at Cos, received part of his schooling there and far surpassed his teachers.

Though he sat under a plane tree at Cos and taught young men rather than ever writing a word, a collection of his case histories and work called the *Corpus Hippocraticum* consists of 72 volumes, and his Hippocratic Oath has had its effect on every medical school graduate. The physician who said that doctors should first of all be kind and discreet and that illness is not a sin is remembered as the Father of Medicine. He found medicine dying in the temple of an outworn religion and touched it with his own devotion to truth.

An Alexandrian born in around the Second Century A.D. is important not so much for what he contributed to the world but as an example of the part an erroneous idea can play in obstructing the development of man. The Alexandrian was Ptolemy—astronomer, mathematician, and geographer.

When Rome supplanted Greece as the source of power in the Mediterranean world economic and political concerns replaced scientific and philosophical inquiry. Greece, bled by Rome of her geniuses, produced no more of their stature, and the center of learning moved from Athens to Alexandria. In the transition the old Greek manner was lost. In Alexandria the grammarian flourished, and form and symbol crushed originality; compilation and criticism took the place of research and deduction. It was as though a thick fog had settled upon the intelligence of man.

Ptolemy, against whom the world still holds a grudge, suits this background because he finalized and stated an ancient idea which suited Biblical lore, an idea just then coming to the West on the lips of Jewish teachers. Ptolemy voiced as final the dictum that the world stands still while the sun and stars revolve around it. This idea appealed to the general conceit that the Earth was by far the greatest and most important thing in the universe. People clung to the Ptolemaic theory. Ptolemy was right on one point: he said that the world was round and that it hung in space with no props to hold it up.

Christianity meshed perfectly with Ptolemy's idea. At that time it was believed that man and the world were the results of a direct and special creation of a Universal Ruler; it was all clear and simple, and man was exalted by his interpretation of nature. The theory congealed into accepted fact. It became a tenet of the church; to doubt it was heresy. No one of importance doubted it—at least publicly—for 14 centuries. 1400 years are a remarkable illustration of the power of a false idea. The church, invincible, monumental, spread itself all through Europe, adding temporal to spiritual power. Dogma supplanted experimentation and creative expression fell before ritual while science slumbered.

In 15th-century Frauenberg lived an old priest-physician who never dreamed of fame. He devoted himself to the care of his parishioners and to his favorite study. The old clergyman believed that he found in his reading of Aristotle the idea that the Earth moved. If Aristotle were correct, he reasoned, then Ptolemy had to be wrong, so he settled down in a sea of figures and in twelve years of mathematical studies he proved to his own satisfaction that the Earth moves. He put his findings in a book and put the book in a trunk.

The shy old scholar's manuscript might have remained in that trunk to this day had not a young doctor come from Wittenburg to visit him. The young man confided his dreams and his doubts to the old physician, and then the old man reluctantly brought his book out of the trunk and showed it to his guest, whose admiring enthusiasm persuaded him to have *De revolutionibus orbimis coelestium* published.

And still the aged cleric had no thought of recognition; he was still satisfied to be a humble servant of humanity. The prospect of having his book published created a fever of excitement which sent him to bed. He hoped the book might be finished soon, but the printing presses were so very slow. Finally the first copy was rushed to his bedside, and the old physician lovingly fondled the pages his eyes could no longer read. Copernicus had joined the band of courageous rebels whose daring, vision, and perseverence had pushed back the curtains of ignorance so that the world might be a better place for humanity.

Copernicus' desire for knowledge was insatiable. Born in 1473 into a German world in which a young man could be either a soldier or a churchman, his vocation was decided by his health and temperament. He pursued the studies of medicine, mathematics, and astronomy in five universities and retired to Frauenberg at the age of twenty-four. In Frauenberg he lived and died as an official of the church, practicing his medicine gratuitously. He did not let his devotion to the church persuade him that the Bible was the source of science. In his day anyone who did not believe that the world stood still at the center of the universe was a hell-bound heretic. This was the heritage Ptolemy left to Europe. Copernicus believed in hell, but he also believed that no one would be damned for using his brain.

When Copernicus yielded to George Joachim's great interest in his book, his health was bad. Grown old in the service of God and man, his years spent in work and thought, he was nearly finished. There was not much the church fathers could do to him, as it seemed most likely that death would soon step in and settle his affairs. He had borne the burdens of half the people of Frauenberg for 30 years and had never thought of himself as a great man, much less that his name would last as long as his planet. E.F.C. Morton wrote, "The dim Titanic figure of the old monk seems to rear itself out of the dull flats around it, pierces with its head the mists that overshadow them and catches the first gleam of the rising sun."

Nearly a century after Copernicus' birth Galileo was born at Pisa, almost within the shadow of the leaning tower. It was 1564 and Italy was bound hand and foot by the traditions of Aristotle. The Inquisition was in its mightiest hour.

One day in the cathedral of Pisa a tall young man stood in the aisle watching the lamps swing back and forth. His fingers were on his pulse; his lips moved; he was counting. For years people watched those lamps swing and few of them ever realized that they were touched by the breath of a great mystery. At that instant Galileo discovered the law of the pendulum and today every ticking watch and every clock gonging the passing of another hour owes its existence to that moment.

His family could not afford to keep him in school, so Galileo whiled away his time by writing about a water balance he had invented and about the center of gravity in solids. In this way he built a reputation which earned him a lectureship at the University of Pisa, where he broke the shackles of tradition by resorting to experimentation. By dropping two objects of unequal weight from the top of the Tower of Pisa he refuted Aristotle's statement that they would reach the ground at different times in direct ratio to their weight. The objects reached the ground simultaneously.

Galileo was appointed professor at Padua. He put his soul and his dynamic personality into his lectures and became popular with the students, whom he often tutored in private. In his voluminous writings appeared the proposal that what is gained in power is lost in speed. In one of his public lectures he embraced and explained the Copernican theory. His colleagues became infuriated at this attempt to reduce the Earth to a mere speck of dust flying around the Sun. The excitement and confusion caused by his statements had barely subsided when news reached him that a

Dutchman had put two lenses together in a way which made distant objects look closer and was using the device as a toy to entertain children at night.

One night the Moon rose over Padua as she had been doing for countless years, but this time she found herself looking down a hollow tube, at the end of which was the eye of Galileo. Galileo explained what he saw through his telescope and people refused to believe him or to look for themselves.

Galileo, undiscouraged, continued to observe. He discovered that Jupiter has moons, and that Venus has phases like those of the Earth's moon. He studied the rings of Saturn. One of the church fathers consoled his flock by saying, "I have read Aristotle many times, and nowhere does he mention spots on the sun. Be assured there are none such."

Finally an impending charge of heresy was brought against Galileo and he went to Rome to clarify his position. By this time he was corresponding with Johannes Kepler, largely on the subject of the Copernican theory. While he was in Rome the church had Copernicus' book banned and demanded that Galileo refrain from teaching the subject, but he tried to skirt their edicts by employing an indirect dialogue form for his next book on the Copernican theory. He was delivered over to the Inquisition and tried for heresy. By the time he recanted he was an old, sick, terrified man.

Galileo's signature could not erase what his eyes had discovered. Though he was placed within the guard of the church, his lifetime habits of work saved him. He wrote the *Dialogue on the New Sciences,* in which he organized his thoughts on mechanics. His work became the basis for Newton's theorems and for the future of the mechanical age. As an old man Galileo reformulated a principle on the pendulum which he had discovered as a boy, and applied it to the measurement of time. He gave the world three laws of motion later reworded by Newton. In his last hours of life the now-blind searcher for truth dictated a treatise on percussion to his secretary.

Galileo's correspondent, Johannes Kepler, was born two days after Christmas, 1571, to poverty, ill health, and domestic unhappiness. He was an imaginative dreamer who lived for the solution of the mystery of Mars, and for a promise he made to a man who befriended him.

Kepler was withdrawn from school by his father, who needed the boy's help in his tavern, but when a chance came to send the frail, studious child to school free of charge, the father agreed. When Kepler finished his university studies he was offered the position of professor of astronomy at

Gratz. He loved mathematics and hated the idea of teaching astronomy, which was then considered to be little better than fortune-telling, but he had to live so he accepted the position.

With a fairness that characterized him, Kepler set about studying astronomy. He developed an intense interest in his subject. He made the planet Mars his obsession, hoping to use it to learn why the stars and planets moved in apparently predetermined courses. He believed that the Sun both drew and repelled the planets. He sent his observations in manuscript form to the great astronomer Tycho Brahe, who was then at Prague, and Tycho suggested that Kepler visit him.

Kepler and Tycho, ill-matched, nevertheless formed a close friendship. Tycho, iconoclastic child of luxury and privilege, was empty of imagination. Kepler was gentle, soft-spoken, and friendly, with rare, beautiful dreams and the perseverance to make them a reality. On his deathbed, Tycho received a promise from Kepler to finish his "Rudolphine Tables."

Lofty titles were bestowed upon Kepler by the courts of Bohemia, Austria, and Rome, but these nations were filling the hands of war from their coffers, and not the hands of human advancement. They left him unpaid, so he was obliged to continue the hated trade of telling fortunes and casting horoscopes to maintain a whining wife.

Kepler accomplished his two treasured dreams. He found the relationship between Mars' distance from the Sun and its speed, and composed a law from his findings; and he published Tycho's "Rudolphine Tables." He studied and wrote on the refraction of light in dense mediums. He heard of Galileo's telescope, and in devising the principle for himself he realized that two convex lenses could be employed to create a real image on which measuring wires could be used. This paved the way for the construction of an accurate astronomical telescope.

For 16 years Kepler sought the exact path in which Mars moved. Eight inches off, he faced the error with these words: "With those eight inches I'll yet unlock the secrets of the heavens." He conceived the idea of an oval orbit instead of the circular orbit in which the Greeks believed. For 16 years he struggled with thousands of numbers on piles of paper until he saw the relationship between two figures. The first expressed the greatest optical inequality of Mars, and the other was half the distance between an ellipse and a circle. He brought to the world the discovery that the planets move in ellipses with the Sun in one focus.

Nothing could stop Johannes Kepler, who stumbled but got back to his feet, who made light of his failures and built from them a tower which brought him closer to the heavens and put celestial laws within his reach. In spite of his fragile body he defied the mysterious universe and in his defiance won an immortal triumph.

The story of science moves portentously, sometimes languidly, sometimes in seven-league boots, through the years. These have been but examples of the great men who loved truth and sought to understand, who created abstract concepts which man was to use to adventure step by step into the unknown. Science is also Pasteur, marveling at the mulberry leaf, marveling at rabies, and then converting his wonder to action and devising the germ theory. Lister then worked out his concepts of sepsis and antisepsis so essential to improvements in surgical techniques for both hospital practice and medical research.

Science is also Einstein, challenging the axiom that a straight line is the shortest distance between points with his concept of relativity, and his magic equation, $E=mc^2$, symbolizing the quality of mass and energy. With that equation the atomic bomb aided the birth of a whole new era. Man, now trembling on the edge of infinity with the power to destroy himself, also has the power to lift himself across the threshold of the physical world into the world of cosmic Consciousness.

The fabricators of this section of the cable are not stilled. Ninety percent of the number of scientists who ever lived are now with us. Knowledge doubles every ten years. In the face of such a mass of knowledge man has invented allies in the form of machines. Man's machines store information and make it instantly available to him, make comparisons and find answers, and are creative.

Man is also beginning to wonder whether he is an adjunct to the machine or the machine an adjunct to man. People are beginning to ask, Who is the master, and who the slave? What are the portents for the future? Men are beginning to conclude that science in itself is not enough, but that science needs values with which man may be constructive, lest it destroy its maker, and itself.

VI

SPIRIT AND ESSENCE

Religion is the third strand in the cable man used to lift himself out of the mud. Science answers questions of "How?" and religion seeks to answer the "Why?" Religion searches for purposes, ends, and values.

There are two aspects of religion. One is its spirit, or essence, and the other is the form the spirit takes, or the institution. The institution is encrusted with human frailties, since it deals, as religion must, with beliefs, practices, feelings, moods, and attitudes. Religion assumes the existence of a Power greater than man, with which man can and does enter into a relationship. It also assumes that the relationship influences man in his day-to-day behavior.

The modern world is so complex and filled with overlapping influences that it is difficult to sort out the ideas which are religious from those which are not. In order to understand the beginnings of religion, ethnologists and anthropologists have studied existing primitive ethnic groups.

The world of the primitive man frequently terrified him. It was a world of powerful forces. He saw that things which moved had life, and he supposed that life to be caused by spirits. His religion is called "animism" because all things were manifestations of spirits, good and bad. How to gain the favor of the good spirits and be protected from the evil ones became a concern which developed into ritual and witchcraft.

There is a concept found to have been common to most of the Pacific region and which has its equivalents in other areas of the world. This concept, an impersonal force called "mana," affects, or is capable of affecting, the affairs of men who seek to control and influence it. It can be conveyed by nearly any medium and spirits can impart it. It shows itself in physical force or in any kind of power or excellence possessed by man. Mana is a force distinguished from the corporal which can act for evil or for good, being thus of great advantage to the individual who possesses and has learned the techniques of controlling it. When this power operates beyond the power of man and outside the ordinary happenings of nature it verges into supernaturalism.

An article in the Hastings *Encyclopedia of Religion and Ethics* entitled "The Art of Mana," by R.R. Maratt, claims that mana was the origin of taboos, because the common people abstained from doing certain things related to the person or subject called mana. When many taboos develop, a division of labor evolves with attendant rituals, creeds, and systems. There are certain ways of obtaining mana and certain ways of disposing of it. In the societies to which it was important, those who had had great amounts of mana were prayed to, and so a god or a series of gods developed. It is therefore believed that the concept of mana was the essential stuff from which magic and religion developed.

The chief difference between magic and religion, at this point, is that religions deal with the social good of the group. Magic is the technique resting on the assumption that the capricious universe and the capricious power governing it can be manipulated and controlled. Religion is the total of man's concepts of his relationships to a higher Power. First, it is a belief in a higher Power; and second, a belief that the Power has to do with or has control over the higher values of man's life, neither of which is of any importance to magic. Magic is related to religion only in that it crops up once in a while in religious worship or ritual.

Religion in whatever form it is found is an attempt to bring man into a harmonious relationship with all the universe through the medium of ideals and standards. True religion is never static; it keeps moving, reaching higher, setting new standards, and replacing old ideals with new. The Bible is a great text outlining this idea. The gradual development of the Hebrew concept of God is a typical example of the pioneering spirit of religion.

VII

RELIGION, THE FLOWER

Civilizations developed their own peculiar pantheons of gods. Worship was performed in rituals appropriate to the time, the place, and the particular spirit, symbol, or deity. Religion has had its pioneers, and one of these individuals who provided an inspiration for mankind was an Egyptian pharaoh whose reign began in or around the year 1375 B.C.

Amenhotep IV, called Ikhnaton, is referred to by Egyptologist James Henry Breasted as the "heretic pharaoh." One of the earliest monotheists, Ikhnaton was a pitifully deformed youth who briefly revolutionized Egyptian art by his insistence upon lifelike portraits, even of himself. He rejected the host of gods and demons because he believed that there was one God over all people, binding them together with love.

In his era there was one particularly powerful

god, Amon, whose priests were corrupt and strong, and Ikhnaton incurred their anger by placing the benevolent sun god Aton in the superior position in state religion, even to the point of including the god's name in his own. He built a new city for Aton, in which he spent 15 years with his famed sister-queen, stately Nefertiti, and their children. The priests of Amon inveighed against him and his concessions to them finally caused Nefertiti to leave him.

Because his doctrines were too advanced for his contemporaries, the reign of Amenhotep IV was brief. At his death the solar religion was abandoned. The new city—the modern town of Amarna—fell into ruin. His body had scarcely been sealed into the tomb when the old contrived religion and the old stylized art were reinstated under his successor, Tutenkhamon.

The fall of Ikhnaton is totally obscure. His name was henceforth obliterated from state documents and a new title, "The Criminal," was selected for him. His crime—and his contribution to the world—was his concept of the unity which he tried to bring from the chaos of innumerable warring supernatural powers.

Abraham was another man to cross the skyline of religious consciousness. There are many theories of the origin of Abraham and his tribes. Dr. Carl

Knopf, in *The Old Testament Speaks* and in his lectures, was of the opinion that Abraham came from the Chaldean capital of Ur and that he was in all probability a contemporary of Hammurabi because, in a letter to Sin-iddinam, Hammurabi mentions the raiders or bandits called the Sa-Gaze, and these marauders may also have been the subject of a letter by Abdi-Hepa of Jerusalem to Amenhotep IV. In this specimen from the Amarna letters they are called Habiri. Abdi-Hepa made the observation that the brigands seemed to come from across the Jordan. From the title Habiri, derived from the verb meaning "crossed over," came the name Hebrew, which is used to refer to the Israelites.

At any rate, Abraham, a tribal chieftain, entered into an area in Canaan where it was the custom to demonstrate one's devotion to God by sacrificing one's first born child. Abraham loved his God and felt that he could do no less, and so he built a pyre of stone and brush on which to lay his son. As he lifted the knife one of the greatest sublimations in history took place. A ram rustled in the brush, and told Abraham in the voice of God that he needed not a dead son, but a living one dedicated to God's purpose. So Abraham substituted the ram for his son. Whether or not the incident would have shown up well on a tape recorder or color film fades to a point of trivia, because Abraham's expression of love influenced the Israelites from that moment on.

Moses is another man of immense religious stature. An incredibly varied collection of individuals influenced him, and though it is only a matter of speculation as to whether Ikhnaton was among them, Moses very likely learned of the concept of monotheism from the records of "The Criminal." The Egyptian princess' foundling child was raised in a pharaoh's court and had access to the archives. He became familiar with the magical tricks of the priests of Amon and could compete with them on an equal level. When he decided to deliver his people from Egyptian bondage he needed all the sleight of hand the priests knew. He matched the priests trick for trick until they, not wanting to take credit for a convenient pestilence, permitted the Hebrews to depart.

Moses had spent the first part of his life in the wilderness, probably in the Sinai Desert east of Egypt. He learned to adjust to the desert environment, so when God called him to lead the people he was prepared. After the passage from Egypt Moses experienced the presence of God on the top of Mt. Sinai and returned to his disorganized people with ten rules of decent human conduct called the Ten Commandments. These were really rules of survival. If men, especially such nomads, were to live socially together, the rules must be observed. When the Israelites prepared to do battle with the Canaanites, they noticed the Canaanite custom of carrying an idol into battle to test its strength. The cautious Israelites carried the Ark of the Covenant with them. When the Ark was captured in battle, they were forced to learn that God could not be contained in an ark or artifact, but that He exists wherever man exists.

Then a solemn procession of prophets followed, exerting its force upon religious history. Each prophet had a doctrine to preach, revealing different aspects of God to those who wrote down Western religious heritage for the purpose of preservation. Amos preached his doctrine of justice and mercy, and Isaiah proclaimed basic principles steadfast in the face of pressures from the East and West. One man deserving of special attention is Hosea.

Biblical scholar, Charles Foster Kent, Ph.D., of Yale, in his book, *The Kings and Prophets of Israel and Judah,* tells this account of Hosea. Hosea had a wife who was unfaithful to him. It was his legal right to put her out of his household and he did so, although he had greatly loved her. The incident did not end there, because Hosea discovered that he could not put her from his heart. Some years later as he passed a slave market he saw his wife put on the auction block to be sold, and the old love welled up in him. He bought her, and, after a probationary period, he reestablished her in his home.

This beautiful story is relatively unimportant when compared to the realization of Hosea afterword: "If I can love Gomer after all her transgressions," he said, "how much greater must God's forgiving love be for the Israelites."

The power of an infinitely forgiving, loving, concerned God blooms into fullness in the life and teachings of Jesus, who told of the Fatherhood of God and the brotherhood of man. Jesus taught that the kingdom of God is in each individual and that God works His powers through men. He said, "I and my Father are one," and "the kingdom of God is within you."

Jesus universalized the Hebrew religious development of a thousand years, and he promised, "... the works that I do shall he [man] do also ...." To those around him Jesus exemplified the idea of what God would be like if He came to Earth. The Israelites understood the relationship of father and son, and Jesus taught them about the universality of God in language they could appreciate.

Jesus would not be considered a great man today because he neither wrote a book nor owned more than the clothes on his back. He loved. He taught in a simple fashion; he opened the door to God.

One of Jesus' adherents was Paul. Paul was a microcosm of the philosophical, religious, and political ideals of the first century. In him met all the major Western traditions of a world rich in cultures. He had a complex personality. Charles Frances Potter likens him to Ikhnaton, whose abnormal body housed an extremely sensitive soul. Paul was short and his legs were crooked, but his spirit was hardy.

Paul was a battlefield for the great contending forces about him. He was a Roman citizen trained as a rabbi, and yet he was impressed by the life and teachings of Jesus. His early youth was spent in Tarsus, which had its advantages. A major commercial center, Tarsus was also a center for religion, particularly the mystic cults, which afforded him the opportunity to study techniques that he put to good use in his later life. He spoke Aramaic, understood the Greek and Roman cultures and their languages, spoke the classic Hebrew in which the scriptures were written, and knew the vulgar Greek of the marketplace. When he quoted the Old Testament he used the Greek version popular among the Jews after their dispersion from Palestine. The great scholar of the first century was Gamaliel, and Paul had the privilege of studying with him.

As a Pharisee, Paul was bent on the destruction of the particular heathen cult called Christianity. He is reported to have had men and women hauled from their houses, imprisoned, and in some cases killed. It is certain that he looked upon his acts as a righteous defense of what he felt to be the true word of God.

He was sent on a mission and on the road to Damascus he had an experience of which the Book of Acts gives three accounts. Whatever happened, Paul indicates in his own writings that he was convinced he had actually seen Jesus, whose followers he was persecuting, and the Book of Acts indicates that he then joined the church at Damascus. He was suspect on both sides because of his background until Barnabas, who was then the head of the Christian Church, accepted him. The earliest writings of Paul, his letters to the Thessalonians, were the first writings of the New Testament.

Because of his continued defiance of the Jewish ceremonial laws, Paul's hosts in Jerusalem proposed that he prove his loyalty by going to the Temple. There he was recognized as the man who had preached against the Jewish law in Asia Minor. This led to the event which caused his arrest and consummated in his martyrdom in Rome. He was saved by the Roman garrison from being beaten to death by an anti-Christian mob, but when the captain commanded the soldiers to take Paul to the fortress Paul spoke to him in Greek. The captain was so surprised that he allowed Paul to address the crowd. Ignoring his own safety, he preached a sermon which can be found, in essence, in Chapter 22 of Acts. The mob called for his death and the captain would have let him be killed, had not Paul claimed Roman citizenship and the right to appeal his case to Rome.

A group of friends, including Luke, were permitted to set sail for Rome with Paul. As they approached Rome, the Christians there heard they were coming and went to meet Paul. The final outcome of Paul's appeal to Rome is not clear. Luke does not describe the execution, and there is some thought that Paul was liberated and went on into Spain, which had been his early plan. There is evidence in the writings of Timothy that he did so and then returned to Rome, at which time the case went against him. In any event, Paul was martyred in Rome about the year 65 A.D.

Paul has been likened to a bridge across which Christianity passed into the Greco-Roman world, and hence into the streams of Western civilization. He found Christianity in the hands of common people who were for the most part uneducated. He was able to develop the basis for a theology that met the needs of the first century and he had the intellectual background and devotion necessary to accomplish the feat.

When the Roman Empire crumbled under the marauding feet of the barbarian Huns, Ostragoths, and Visigoths, official state stability became a responsibility of the church. State institutions were replaced by the great bishoprics. The citizenry grumbled that the spoliation of Rome happened because the ancient gods were no longer revered. During the 800 years of Rome's paganism nothing like this had happened, but Rome's partial embrace of Christianity had occasioned upheaval, they charged.

At this moment in history in the fourth century a solitary monk on the north coast of Africa picked up his pen and wrote a book called *The City of God*. The monk was the Bishop of Hippo, known to history as St. Augustine. He became the architect for the medieval church which managed to hold together the minds, souls, and aspirations of men during the Dark Ages.

Then some of the old writings were found, among them the works of Plato and Aristotle. The school of Neoplatonism was born and men were made restless. The Renaissance dawned, and

Neoplatonism threatened ancient beliefs. At this juncture another churchman put forth his Christian philosophy and doctrine and he, St. Thomas Aquinas, became the author of much modern religious thought. His ideas are still a potent influence.

St. Thomas Aquinas was born in 1225. His mother, the Countess Theodora, heard the annunciation of Bonus, a hermit, who told her, "Rejoice, O Lady, for thou art with child. Thou shalt bring forth a son whom thou shalt call Thomas." When Thomas was three an earthquake and a terrific electrical storm swept over Naples. As he played with his sister, she was struck and killed by a bolt of lightning. It appeared to his family that his life had been miraculously spared and that God must have some divine plan for his future, and so, when he was five, the count and countess dedicated his life to God and the Benedictine monks provided his education.

The Benedictine abbey of Monte Cassino was severe in its discipline and the monks were required to be devout and prayerful. All activity and conversation centered on thoughts of God. Tradition has it that young Thomas, though a brilliant scholar, plagued his teachers with the constant query, "What is God? What is God?" At 16 Thomas joined the Dominican order of friars, which took to the city streets together with the Franciscan order and became known as the teaching and preaching friars.

It was the age of the revival of learning. The Crusades had loosened the stones of the medieval cloister and learning was removed from the monastery to a more worldly struggle between Greek philosophy, Christian theology, and the sciences imported from Arabia. The Dominicans were far removed from the wealthy, cloistered, powerful Benedictines. Dedicated to working among men, they begged their way through the world, owning no property of their own. As a Dominican, Thomas renounced his worldly goods and his right to inherit the title of count. He took the solemn Dominican oaths of poverty and was sent first to Rome, and then to Paris.

In the Christmas season of 1244 Thomas set out for Paris and Cologne with John of Germany, head of the Dominican order, for the purpose of studying under Albertus Magnus. That great teacher, at the height of his power as a master of theological and secular learning, was to shape the major portion of young Thomas' life. The quiet boy, with his large size and broad forehead, made such a contrast to his noisy classmates that he was nicknamed "the dumb ox from Sicily." Thomas remained serene under the taunts and once, given a thesis to defend by his illustrious teacher, did the work so ably and completely that Albertus said, "We call this young man a dumb ox, but he will one day fill the world with his bellowing."

Thomas distinguished himself in 1255 by successfully pleading the case of the Dominican order before the Pope. He received his Doctor of Divinity the next year and continued thereafter to teach in Paris and lecture to the University of the Papal Court, a traveling school which accompanied the Pope on his tours of Italy.

On his way to the Council of Lyon, Thomas Aquinas fell ill and died in the Distercian abbey of Fossa Nuova. It was March 7, 1274. The quarrel over his body resulted in the curious compromise of severing its members, most of which were interred in Rome, though Salerno and Naples received portions, and the right arm was sent to Paris. He was canonized in 1323, and in 1567 Pope Pius V pronounced St. Thomas Aquinas to be one of the five "Doctors of the Church."

St. Thomas Aquinas is considered by many to be the patron saint of the Roman Catholic educational institution. He produced 35 octaval volumes of the highest quality. In these works he summarized the theology and the philosophy of his day but organized along a different line, which formed a backbone of Roman Catholic teaching for centuries. He did his best to create a synthesis of the science and religion of his time.

There are men who believe that God went on a holiday when the Bible was completed. They fail to appreciate the conditions which brought the books of the Bible into existence. In the early centuries of the Christian era an individual who wanted to attract attention to his thoughts would write an article to which he would sign an Apostle's name, or in which he would pretend to be quoting one of the Gospels. The world became burdened with spurious writings. The church fathers met to determine the originals from the copyists, and thus the New Testament came into being.

Fortunately, God did not stop inspiring people. There were the great theologians of the Renaissance and the Reformation: Martin Luther, John Knox, John Wesley, Roger Williams. Each of these followed doctrinal differences, an outgrowth of the Reformation. Then about two centuries ago there began to move in the minds of men an idea which always seemed to be the result of political revolution. There have long been questions whether political structure influences theology or whether theology influences political structure. In other words, does religion follow politics, or do political structures follow religion? In the early days they talked about God, or God of Hosts, King of Kings, but the idea of equality of mankind began to stir in the soul of the people. The idea of democracy was beginning to develop, ready to stand in the political tumult of nationalistic struggle.

In the early 1800s there was a counterpart of this in a new phase of democratizing God. These early pioneers of New Thought did not start out to do that, nor did their followers realize the long-range significance of their teaching.

Phineas Parkhurst Quimby was born February 16, 1802 in Lebanon, New Hampshire. He became an itinerant clock maker in Belfast, Maine, but he was an independent and original thinker.

Quimby had a physical ailment which was pronounced incurable by the physicians of his time. So he set out to find a cure. He first studied mesmerism as a therapeutic remedy, but soon gave this up. He did find a technique by which he restored himself to health. He said, "If it has helped me why can't it help others?" He analyzed his method, reduced it to a few simple principles, and tried to find the underlying cause of sickness in general.

Many people came to him to be cured, some for instruction, and some remained as students. Such great names in the field of New Thought are: Julius Dressler and his wife; Rev. Warren Felt Evans, identified with the Swedenborg Movement; and Mary Baker Eddy, who came first to be cured and then to be a student, and later founded Christian Science. The teachings of Mary Baker Eddy are fully explained in *Science and Health with Key to the Scriptures,* and have brought relief and comfort to millions of people.

Quimby taught that God is immanent in man; that God is eternal, everlasting, and that everything physical in the natural world is a manifestation of the spiritual world, the world of causes. He taught that our thought is an instrument of Divine Mind. He did not feel that the world was an illusion, but it was rather an expression of Divine Mind. He did not deny disease. He said that sickness is due largely to the mental and spiritual complex. He expanded this at times by saying that false religions and primitive medical teachings gradually built up what he called a mental psychic knot, which interfered with the natural functions of the body organism. This was 50 years before Freud and Jung came on the scene of teaching and healing. It was his feeling and conviction that erroneous thought, morbid emotions, worries about the future, remorse over past fears, suppressed desires and hopes, all externalized themselves in bodily conditions of ill health and disease.

Quimby's method was to assist the patient to discover what the knot is and then to untie it. He explained to the patient the mental or spiritual cause of the ailment, and as he said, "The explanation is the cure."

Then in the 1860s Ralph Waldo Emerson came on the stage at just the right time. He was known as the great transcendentalist. He taught that God is immanent as well as transcendent. He influenced greatly the New Thought teachers who followed.

Charles and Myrtle Fillmore, after a series of dramatic healings, founded the Unity School of Christianity, a school of religion whose influence is felt around the world, and established *Unity Magazine*.

The man who climaxed this long parade of religious explorers and pioneers is almost contemporary in the modern world. Ernest Holmes, again a New Englander, was a courageous thinker, an individualist, a great lecturer, and an insatiable reader and scholar. Ernest Holmes established the Institute of Religious Science, *Science of Mind* Magazine, and the Church of Religious Science, which later divided into the International Association of Religious Science Churches and the United Church of Religious Science. He headed this latter organization until he made the great transition. As he said many times in his development of Science of Mind, it "sought to collect the facts of science, the opinions of philosophy, and the revelations of religion." He taught that God is not out in the external world on a cloud, but God is the innermost Consciousness of man; that the Science of Mind is a study of the Power back of creation. He taught that the Universe never plays favorites. There are certain universal laws that work in the physical world, and there are laws that work in the mental and spiritual world as well.

To him, prayer was "a movement of thought, within the mind of the one praying, along a definite line of meditation; that is, for a specific purpose."

No one knows exactly what Mind is, but we do study what It does. We discover It's laws, and we learn to work with them. The salvation of man lies within himself. This whole new trend frees man from superstition, from fear, and provides a method by which he may forgive himself and learn to love himself if he would love his neighbor.

In describing Religious Science Ernest Holmes wrote: "The thought of the ages has looked to the day when science and religion shall walk hand in hand through the visible to the invisible. A movement which endeavors to unify the great conclusions of human experience must be kept free from petty ideas, from personal ambitions, and from any attempt to promote one man's opinion. Science knows nothing of opinion but recognizes a government of law whose principles are universal. These laws, when complied with, respond alike to all. Religion becomes dogmatic and often superstitious when based on the lengthened shadow of any one personality. Philosophy intrigues us only to the extent that it sounds a universal note."

God is still inspiring great poems, important plays, fine books, and worthy conduct. He is present in the lines of Keats and Tennyson, Browning and T. S. Eliot, and in the research of scientists and the teaching of theologians; He works through the lives of Paul Tillich, Lecomte du Noüy, Pierre Teilard de Chardin, and all the simple folk who carry their daily burdens and provide their fellows with inspiration and strength. Chapters of the living Bible walk the roads today. "Be careful," someone cautioned, "because you may be the only Bible someone is reading." According to modern science, each individual is becoming more and more an expression of infinite Wisdom which makes man a sensitive expression of the Universe. God is at work today in the manifold expressions of goodness, beauty, and truth which are first Universal, and then personalized.

VIII

THE ENDLESS JOURNEY

Three great forces have been at work on the looms of time creating the fabrics of today and the designs of tomorrow. Law, serving as a conservator, prevents too rapid progress or retrogression, and acts to achieve stability by regulating power. Science pushes out in all directions, asking questions, gathering information and occasionally finding an answer. Religion attempts to explain the why of things, and underscores values, creates standards, and attempts to help man find his place in the Universe. By law, science, and religion man has arrived at the place from where he contemplates the potential of himself and the immensity of Eternity.

There is a tremendous unity to the whole picture of man and his past. He is, in a sense, the fluorescence of six billion years, and, immediately, of almost two million years of slow development and change, adaptation, trial and error, failure and success. Man is just a baby learning to walk on the Earth, which is a mere speck in this great universe.

Sir James Jeans tried to help us visualize the relationship of man to his solar system with a little chart. On the chart is a ball one inch in diameter, representing the Earth. 232 yards away is another ball nine feet in diameter, and that is the Sun. A third ball is close to the Earth, the Moon, the size of a cranberry. According to this scale the nearest star would be 40,000 miles in space. On that tiny one-inch ball is a speck so infinitesimal that it cannot be physically represented, and yet you and I know very well that it is there. It is you, and it is I.

We are more than organisms, or protoplasm, or chemicals. We are possessed of a miraculous time-enduring energy called Life. It is synthesizing, compounding, creative, and limitless. The qualities of kindness and goodness, beauty, truth, and love we see expressed by man at his finest are a glimpse of the infinite God, because man and God are one—they live in each other as water in sponges, as sponges in water. Man is the finite expression of the Infinite. God is immanent, but God is also transcendent.

Carl Sumner Knopf used to say that man and civilization go through three distinct stages: first,

"What's mine is mine if I can keep it;" second, "What's yours is mine if I can get it;" and third, "What's mine is yours if I can share it." When man arrives at the third stage he is truly civilized. He has, at that stage, developed qualities of character and personality that make him uniquely human. He has a potential for greatness. He has the ability to think, to dream, to remember yesterday, to orient to today, and to contemplate a better tomorrow. He is creative; above all, he can love, and he is capable of receiving love. These are the qualities which have lifted man out of the past. To each man is given a few years of life and the opportunity to build something that gives worth to existence.

Emerson wrote, "Nothing divine dies. All good is eternally reproductive. The beauty of nature reforms itself in the mind, and not for barren contemplation, but for new creation . . . . Every spirit builds itself a house; and beyond its house a world; and beyond its world, a heaven. Know, then, that the world exists for you. For you is the phenomenon perfect. What we are, that only can we see. All that Adam had, all that Caesar could, you have and can do. Adam called his house, heaven and earth; Caesar called his house, Rome; you perhaps call yours, a cobbler's trade; a hundred acres of ploughed land; or a scholar's garret. Yet, line for line and point for point, your dominion is as great as theirs, though without fine names. Build, therefore, your own world."

There is a story about a castle with an enchanted casement. Certain people who climbed the stairs and looked out the casement window would see children dancing and singing, with flowers woven in their hair. From the same window other people saw creeping vermin and vile decay. Then a scholar who had delved into the records of the time in which the castle was built visited it and told this story. It was built by a duke who was greatly loved in the community. He was very kind and understanding, and each person in the area wished to make a contribution to his castle. So each brought something that represented his craft. The glazier brought a piece of window glass into which he had put skills long since forgotten. Such a polish did he put on the glass that when a person looked through it he saw not the outside world but his own innermost thoughts.

"God enters by a private door into every individual," Emerson observed.

Man creates his own obstacles to fuller living when he permits himself to exercise fear, hate, prejudice, worry, or indecision in an unconstructive manner. Certain aspects of fear and worry are constructive. Yet achievement can be halted by fear, worry, and indecision, which cause loss of time and the will to achieve. Hate injures the one who hates more than it does the object of hatred, and prejudice acts similarly to make the bigot despise something he does not understand.

On the other hand, man possesses the power to bring life to fulfillment for himself. He can exercise an appreciation for himself and other men—the microcosm; and for the universe and its animate and inanimate beings—the macrocosm. He can have faith; man cannot live in the modern world without faith. Faith in man and his world and faith in God are necessary.

Happiness is necessary. The man who looks for trouble usually finds it, and the man who talks about trouble usually has a lot to talk about. Our thoughts are similar to magnets and attract like-nesses in our experience. Thoughts are reflected in our future; they can change our appearance. Someone has said that the gods we worship write their names on our faces. Not everyone can be beautiful, but all can be pleasant. There was a little girl who knelt to pray one night and said, "Dear God, make all the bad people good and all the good people pleasant." Happiness is its own re-ward, and we are as happy as we determine to be. Happiness brings bloom to life, meaning to experi-ence, and richness to memories. An Indiana schoolteacher said, "Happiness consists of three things: someone to love, something to do, and something to look forward to."

Life is a venture, a journey, as Tennyson put it, "whose skylines fade forever and forever as we move." We expose our minds to beautiful thoughts, beautiful music, beautiful paintings and scenery, and these bring out qualities of harmony, goodness, and truth from the depths of eternal cosmic Consciousness which is within us.

Emerson wrote: "The scholar of the first age received into him the world around; brooded thereon; gave it the new arrangement of his own mind, and uttered it again. It came into him life; it went out from him truth. It came to him shortlived actions; it went out from him immortal thoughts. It came to him business; it went from him poetry. It was dead fact; now, it is quick thought. It can stand and it can go. It now endures, it now flies, it now inspires. Precisely in proportion to the depth of mind from which it issued, so high does it soar, so long does it sing."

The use of leisure time is a force that leads the way to heaven or to hell. The interests that we develop stimulate the growth of creative power, or they stultify, depress, and retard. We freely select our associates and from our associations come friends, who have a way of building themselves into the fiber and marrow of our being.

It is a wonderful and thrilling experience to be a human being in this modern world, where so much is known about the past and about what we are. We realize that we stand on the threshold of Eternity. Scientists with electronically attenuated eyes and ears listen to the heartbeat of the Earth and peer out into the infinite, discern the murmurings of the cosmos, the symphony of the swinging spheres, and the unity of all things.

The full life can be captured by being consciously aware of God's presence within us. Here for a few brief years each is given a claylike substance—who knows but what it is a cocoon in which the eternal Essence of the soul resides and at the appropriate time will emerge into infinite beauty and glory and love.

Here and there across the plain of centuries stands a giant. Sometimes his feet are buried in the blistering sands of confusion and persecution, sometimes he is drinking a cup of hemlock, and at other times he is wearing a wreath of thorns and is nailed upon a cross. Yet these individuals had one thing in common. They spoke a common language and they wooed humanity into a more divine expression of Life. As Chico put it in the motion picture *Seventh Heaven:* "There is a ladder from the sewer to the stars for those who wish to climb."

Who, therefore, can say the old Bishop was wrong when, holding a clot of mud in one hand and a white flower in the other, he said, "Beautiful mud!"